AF269848

Meet a Snowy Owl

Katie Peters

GRL Consultant Diane Craig,
Certified Literacy Specialist

Lerner Publications ◆ Minneapolis

Lerner Publications
An imprint of Lerner Publishing Group, Inc.
241 First Avenue North
Minneapolis, MN 55401 USA

For reading levels and more information, look up this title at www.lernerbooks.com.

Main body text set in Memphis Pro 24/39
Typeface provided by Linotype.

Photo Acknowledgments
The images in this book are used with the permission of: © Jim Cumming/Shutterstock
Images, pp. 3, 8–9, 16 (center); © Valeriya Starovoitova/Shutterstock Images, pp. 4–5, 16
(left); © Guoqiang Xue/Shutterstock Images, pp. 6–7, 16 (right); © RT Images/Shutterstock
Images, pp. 10–11; © Natalliaskn/Shutterstock Images, pp. 12–13; © Emojibb.Family/Adobe
Stock, pp. 14–15.

Front cover: © nik7ch/Shutterstock Images

Library of Congress Cataloging-in-Publication Data

Names: Peters, Katie, author.
Title: Meet a snowy owl / Katie Peters.
Description: Minneapolis : Lerner Publications, [2025] | Series: Let's look at polar animals
    (pull ahead readers - nonfiction) | Includes index. | Audience: Ages 4–7 | Audience:
    Grades K–1 | Summary: "Snowy owls are beautiful creatures with many neat features
    and traits. Colorful photographs and leveled text give readers an up-close look at these
    polar birds. Pairs with the fiction title, Owen's Feathers"—Provided by publisher.
Identifiers: LCCN 2023031819 (print) | LCCN 2023031820 (ebook) | ISBN 9798765626337
    (library binding) | ISBN 9798765629321 (paperback) | ISBN 9798765634646 (epub)
Subjects: LCSH: Snowy owl—Juvenile literature.
Classification: LCC QL696.S83 P425 2025 (print) | LCC QL696.S83 (ebook) | DDC 598.9/7—
    dc23/eng/20230713

LC record available at https://lccn.loc.gov/2023031819
LC ebook record available at https://lccn.loc.gov/2023031820

Manufactured in the United States of America
1 – CG – 7/15/24

Table of Contents

Meet a
Snowy Owl

The owl has two eyes.

The owl has two wings.

The owl has two legs.

The owl has two feet.

The owl has two eggs.

Now the owl has two babies!

Did You See It?

eyes

legs

wings

Index